Horsemanship by Osmosis

Tess Delaney

DEDICATION

To those who suffered for my horses

CONTENTS

ACKNOWLEDGMENTS

Mum, Rick, Dad, Wendy, Kino, Albee, Jimmy

Thank You ☺

1 The Originals

The freezing shards of wind scratched at my ears, as I stared at the scruffiest ponies in the world. Before that day I didn't know that horses could get dreadlocks on their backs, and I didn't know that horses could be that skinny and still stand up. The chestnut one reminded me of my friend Pete. The other one was just.. Well.. Tiny. The man shrugged. Yours if you want them. I didn't really. They were a right state. Not quite what I'd had in mind over the years of dreaming of lofty horse ownership. Didn't look very gymkhana to me. But there was no way I could leave them on that hillside, because they were looking at me like they expected something. And that's how this stuff starts.. Innocently.. Without even noticing.. By osmosis...

So I put the stupid horses in the back of my Renault Master. Not a horse lorry Renault Master. Just a Renault Master. I bribed them in with some hay I'd picked up. Amazingly, the little white fella piled right in. The nonchalant skinny one that reminded me of Pete just sort of followed. I shut the door. See? Said the bloke. You're a horse whisperer. I can't even catch them.

It wasn't until later I realised that it's cos they'd got my number as a mug, even before I knew I was one. They came over, they sniffed my hand, they let me put halters on, and they got in the van. That's what's s'posed to happen isn't it? I didn't know any different.

We drove home past Newgale, with the Pete horse's nose stuck between the seats like a dog, checking out the landscape. While the tiny white one fretted and mithered and whinged about being tied up. Don't blame him, I thought. Eat some hay horse. We'll be home soon.

Amazingly, they both had passports. I guess if you're going to dump a couple of five month olds at the Llanybydder sales then you're going to need a passport. The guy I got them off had picked them up from the sales in November. He said it was commonplace that people came and picked up the foals that were left and took them so that the meat man didn't get them. I've never been to the sales at Llanybydder, and I never will. I have been told it's a good day out by people that profess to love horses, which made no sense to me then and makes no sense to me now. So anyway, these little guys had been stuck in a field with an ex-racehorse and a little pony and six months later I came along, after seeing an ad in the Friday Ad. The field was on the headland near Whitesands, freezing enough in June, let alone all winter. I felt so sorry that these little guys had had to fend for themselves at such an young age. I still can't read War Horse, because I can't get past the first three pages, where the horsey is taken from his mummy. My heart aches for all of them that it happens to, and I realise now it happens a lot. All the bloody time.

The ginger Pete horse was called Gold Dust on his passport. A far cry from the matted, emaciated, barely a horse looking thing that barely stood before me. I wondered what to call the poor fella. He looked at me, I looked at him back. I had just read Groucho Marx's autobiography, and in there, when telling a sensitive story about some MGM boss or famous actor, he'd be loathe to call them by their real names, so instead, he would say "we'll call him Delaney." I guess that makes sense, I thought. We'll call him Delaney. The little white one, who according to his passport is actually palomino, but really he's just a bit nicotine yellow, and looks white until standing next to a proper white horse, was called Myrddin. Less silly than Gold Dust, but still a bit pretentious pony ring. I bastardised his name to Smurf. And so, with no planning and with absolutely no idea what I was doing, I became a mother of colts. My horsey friends said I was mad. Green on green equals black and blue they said. Well yes.. I said.. But I'm not gonna be riding yearlings am I? We'll learn together. Oh, how they laughed.

It took, literally, months to get near the boys. Delaney came round more quickly than Smurf, and seemed an old soul in an old body. Smurf was flighty, scared, angry, annoyed and suspicious.

Everyone raved about how beautiful he was. No one ever called Delaney beautiful, because quite frankly, he looked as rough as a badger. His shoulders stuck out at funny angles, his legs were gangly, his nose was Roman. Everyone loved Smurfs nose... Smurf had that dish nose that everyone loves, later I learned that this was because of the Arabian stallions that were, in years past, sent to run on the mountains with the Welsh mountain mares.

I often look back and think about just how scared I was of them. They would wander close by while I was sitting on the grass, and invariably I would get up and move, fearing that for absolutely no reason they'd see fit to kick me in the face. You hear the stories; the little girl who was kicked in the head and killed. The girl who fell in Broadmoor when we were in primary school, a girl called Adele Wisdom. She was a bit older than us. She and used to win all the sports day stuff. She was riding a horse and I think maybe a car was involved. She was 11.

These stories, along with earlier experiences I'd had with and around horses, didn't help me in my quest to get all fearless around Smurf and Delaney. When I was young, some friends of mine used to go to the stables and get hire ponies for the winter. I always found this concept a bit terrifying. Could no one else see this as an accident waiting to happen? Thankfully, in that circle of friends nothing did happen, although a girl from the village who I'd never known, was kicked in the head and killed. Or she fell off. I don't remember. Her dad always hated horses after that. It was a story when we moved to the village, played out long before we got there. But the sullen, pained expression on her dad's face was an unspoken fact of the village. She became one of the ghosts of the community, along with the two boys killed on a motorbike years later. Horses were in the same league as motorbikes, although statistically, you're 20 times more likely to be killed by a horse than a motorbike.

One afternoon as I stood near Smurf he suddenly swung his butt towards me. The years of warnings from horsey friends about kicks and death and disability turboed through my consciousness. In slow motion my untrained mind searched for some sort of residual knowledge to connect with, some clue as to how to react. Without thinking, instinctively, with the sense of survival of my ancestors and almost without daring to hope, I scratched his butt. Smurf stopped. I heard him think about kicking me and then I felt a snap in the air, a change in the atmosphere, almost a zap of electricity surging and going to ground. The moment hung there waiting for something to happen. I kept on scratching. Smurf stood and let himself be scratched, and there was flicker of recognition in his eye as it turned backwards in my direction. I don't know how long I stood there and scratched. It could have been twenty years or twenty seconds. But when I stopped, Smurf was my friend.

Since that day, and with every horse I've met since there has always been a version of that moment. It's not always associated with scratchy bums, which has become the staple diet of the deli-repertoire, but there is always a moment where, as some old playwright once said, we turned a strange corner. Sometimes it happens in seconds. Sometimes it takes years. It depends on a lot of things, but it always happens. There have been a couple of occasions where I thought it never would. It's difficult to explain, but it's just a moment of, well hello there horsey. There you are. And yes, here I am. That's it. That's all there is. There's nothing else, no tricks, no anything. Not a gimmick in sight, and no ulterior motives. I find myself a little bit addicted and overwhelmed by this moment. When it happens a joyous adrenaline tips me over the edge and I gush with lovingness and softness, and then I have a bit of a breakdown for allowing myself to get all hippy about everything. However, much as I'd like to deny any sense of higher feeling, religious type illumination, libatious pourings or cleansing of spirit, I can't, because it's there, and it happens. And the fact that it happened that day made me realise just how dependent on these beings I was going to become. That monumental moment with Smurf became the litmus and the confidence for all of the moments since. I'd had it before but didn't know. I had met other horses and felt that they were pleading, and put it down to my overactive mind and a past as a rather arduous animal rights campaigner. I think back now and I know what they were saying. I knew then, but didn't trust it. Didn't trust me, didn't trust them; all this mistrust all over the place, and there was me thinking it was all a matter of going all out and learning everything. Not just everything, but everything to the point of ridiculous obsession. This is how I operate, it's always been the same, and it always will be. I made it my business to learn everything there was to know as quickly as possible, and nail this horsey thing like a boss. Delaney, a Section C part bred mountain pony, would grow big enough to ride. Smurf the tiny, being an iddy biddy section A, who in a parallel universe would have been destined to become the standard issue, hectic, small, bitey, child's pony, would instead earn his keep in a cart and look cute. I had it all worked out. So what I needed, was a horse that I could ride now. One that would teach me what I needed to know. One that would show me how to deal with these little boys as they grew up. One that would look after me and carry me over the hills whilst Ding and Dong flitted behind like a flaxen, golden stallion and a fluffy, slightly palomino unicorn, their manes slicing the air as they reared and frolicked. Yep. I needed a riding horse.

2. Cali

She had the best fringe I'd ever seen. I'd decided already as we drove into the yard and saw her peeping from a stable, but I went through the motions of looking at the others. They were out in the field, and friendly enough, but not all cuddly like that fluffy one inside, the one with the epic fringe. Now I have since learned (there's gonna be lot of this), that in law enforcement this is called a clue. It didn't occur to me why this one was in and those ones were out. I loved her, and made an arrangement to come back and ride.

They say that horses choose you. Is that true? With Cali I can't decide if that was or wasn't the case. I rode her a couple of times, and to be fair, I absolutely crapped myself. She turned quickly, didn't want you to mount, shook her head, ran off at a trot for little other reason than she could, and that she knew there wasn't much you can do about it. Being groomed didn't seem a problem. Being tacked up didn't either. She was pretty good with getting her feet picked up. She accepted all procedure. Right up until you my tried to get on. And then the arse would swing away and mounting became an event. Once on, her panic response set in, which meant so did mine. One day, after I'd given the bloke 800 quid for her, with the added bonus that he threw in a few months of free livery with the use of an indoor school (again, a clue), I got on Cali and cried. Just cried my eyes out. My friend Rachel was with me, one of the friends who had always had a Norchard winter pony back in the day, a stubborn grey called Polly who used to dump me every time I had a go on her.

"What's up Tessie?"

I choked and sobbed and forced the words out; "I love her so much, but she scares me to death."

Rach looked at me in that cynical, *oh for God's sake, Auntie Tessie* way that she always does when I'm being a pathetic numpty. "Why do you want horses if you're scared of them?"

Excellent question, I thought. I wasn't sure why. I'd always wanted horses. There seemed no other way of being to be. But I didn't go horse riding or get a winter pony. That seemed like lots of getting up early, falling off, and dealing with the mean girls that frequented such establishments. I was busy mooning around the village graveyards and riding my bike to the beach. But I often hung out with my friends and their horses. They would fall about as one of their usually sedentary equines would run off with me. Tiger, Emma's pony, took me all the way up from the beach to the castle, as I screamed for help and the others tried not to wet themselves. We used to jump Polly in the field. Well.. Rachel did. I used to drop off the side the minute she lifted her front hooves. It all seemed very difficult and dangerous, and fun, but… like..

what have we all got? Death wishes? These kids were a lot younger than me, and I wasn't very old. 9, 10, 11 year olds, being given horses to care for on their own. And fair play to them, they got jobs and bought hay and rode and did all sorts of horsey things. Two of them now work with horses and never stopped riding. One of them owns a show yard. They worked hard and they got their rewards and they kept the love for a lifetime. But I still didn't get it. The bit I liked was standing in the field while they all grazed and larked around. Not the kids. The horses. I always wondered what their opinion of that metal in their mouth was, or how they felt about someone climbing on them. My buddies were fearless, and hoolied off without a care in the world. Perhaps, deep down, I've always been little miss risk assessment, probably a throwback to the days when my grandad was too afraid to let me leave the house because every time I did I ended up hurting myself. The nurses at the hospital knew me on sight. They called me Calamity Jane. I was always a bit accident prone. So, why did I want to get involved with these animals that I spent all my time worrying were going to kill my friends? What was it I liked? Why didn't I want a Norchard pony? Well... One.. They weren't yours. They were on loan. And I didn't understand the concept of having to give it back. Seriously? Give it back? Once you loved it? How does that work? What if I don't? I'd have to run away from home and take the horse. Plus, every time I rode, I fell off. And I didn't get hurt, but I got scared I guess. It didn't have the same appeal to it as all those years before when I'd put reins on my bicycle and on the garden gate and on the dog or anything else I could find. I tried to turn my sheepdog into a horse and cart with a lead and a pair of roller skates once. That was a disaster right there. I put it down to it being the wrong kind of dog.

So here was my dilemma presented to me. What did I want horses for? Well to ride, obviously that's why I bought Cali, but here was me, all scaredy cat. Rach could ride her, but she looked like the unhappiest horse in the world going round and round. I insisted on not keeping my reins tight, convinced that contact meant hurt, and the natural progression was a well honed plan to switch to a rope halter. All this before I'd learned to stay on.

I had been going to college to do an NVQ in equine studies and the BHS exams. There was riding involved in that, and I did pretty well on the horses that are ridden all the time. Although I was perpetually told off for not tightening my reins, or for singing to the horse, or going one handed with California reins, and I argued incessantly with the tutor about ulcers and hay and horse diets and scratchy bums, and wasn't very popular at all. Luckily for all concerned I slipped a disc in my back and made the decision to stop going. I was relieved. All this which hand to use whilst grooming stuff drove me nuts. And take the horses away from their hay and tie them, bored, while you do stuff? Why? What's that all about? Why not let them just eat their hay? Then you don't have to tie them, and piss around with head collars and bridles and lead ropes. I didn't understand any of the reasons we were taught to do things the way we were. It just all seemed to be an arse-about-face way of trying to keep the horseperson safe while simultaneously exposing him to as many risky situations as possible in an enclosed area. I will unequivocally state here, on the record, that the BHS way of horsemanship makes absolutely no sense to me at all whatsoever. These things were tasks invented by army leaders to keep the cavalry soldiers busy. That's it. Why are these outmoded, older concepts still in use? Why are little kids still getting kicked by tied up ponies at riding clubs while they faff around annoying the horse?

One thing college did do though, was improve my riding to the point that getting on Cali no longer resulted in a heart attack. Just a panic attack, anxiety attack, or as time went on, no attacks at all, just a faint nervousness that never really went away. I had mustered the guts to get on her with just a rope halter, and we had been going for walks and basically doing some chumming up. Walking in hand was something we established when she was on livery, before being brought home. The first time I took her out up the road she was a bit barmy , but I just kind of dealt with her like I would a dog. Let her have a sniff, a munch. She wanted to go that way, so I'd turn her in a circle, and we'd go my way, and then back her way again, but we got to the end of the track and came back again, of course at a much easier pace. When I got back the yard owner was standing by the stables looking surprised.

"You been for a walk?"

"Aye."

He paused. "Last woman who tried that came back ten minutes after the horse with no skin on her hands."

I wondered why he hadn't told me that before the eight hundred nicker, but then I'd already sussed out that this was not an easy horse. Rach said she had potential to be a wonderful ridden horse, and with that in mind I had set about that very mission, albeit my way, with a rope halter. I said that my aim was to ride her in a rope halter round the fields. That was all I wanted. *No chance*. Said everybody who knew horses. *Why not*? I asked. Heads were shook, teeth were sucked, tuttings occurred, and generally I was lampooned for being an eejit. By now, I had started to find out little things about Cali. She'd been sent to so and so and called too unpredictable. She'd been loaned by blah blah, and then blah blah, and then oojimeh, etc, etc. She'd basically been passed around and around until she did something to upset all the whoever they weres. And then one day, at a funeral, my sons friend, an extremely good rider, who had a reputation for getting on anything and handling it came up to me and said; "You've got Cali haven't you?"

"Er.. Yes.. I have." I could tell by her tone it was a comment towards the more ominous. "Why?"

"That horse bucked me so hard that I haven't been on a horse since."

"Oh." I said.

Her comment followed me all the way to the weekend. Me and Cali had worked quite a lot on catching, and through it was always preceded by a little dance it was usually quite quickly do-able. This day she wasn't having any of it. I followed her around, doing all my best pressure/release stuff that I'd learned on internets after thousands of hours watching everyone in the whole world working with horses. She moved, I moved, in, out, shake it all about. No chance, she said. Eventually, Cali complied.

Next was getting tacked up and on. Tack. Yeh OK. She did the thing. Getting on? Ha! Out went the arse. *You can kinda kiss this my friend. You ain't getting on.*
I bloody am Cal, I said.
You're bloody not, said Cal. And on it went.

Eventually, she stood, and I got on. A bit hot and bothered, a bit irritated. I wanted to ride nicely, not give a bad rendition of *One Man and his Dog*. Walk on, horse face. I gave the girl a nudge. She walked. About ten feet. I felt a tension, a spike, a still moment of air, as Cali put her weight full onto her hindquarters and launched herself into what I thought was going to be a sudden gallop, but which turned out to be an exploding wrench of a buck which took me completely by surprise and sent me careering into space and finally landing heavily on my side, crushing my old frame like those caravans on Top Gear that they used to drop from great heights. Cali bounced off and landed in the corner of the temporary pen, breathing heavily. I got up, was pleased to note that I could,

You know what you're gonna have to do now don't you?
I looked at Cali. She looked at me back.
Christ. Aye. I gotta get back on.

OK. Where did that rule come from? Is it for the horse? Or for the human? Why do we feel so compelled to repeat the trauma that just occurred. Are we letting the horse get away with it? Is he learning bad lessons? Are we extolling our superiority? What's it all about? That's all rhetorical by the way. I've heard all the answers that people give to those question. It's the same one they give for all other questions. *You gotta show that horse who's boss.*

I led her to the mounting block. Jesus Christ, said Cal. Are you freaking serious, human? She moved her butt. But only once. Then she dutifully let me get back on. I took a few steps and quickly bailed, calling her all the good girls, ripped off all her tack and let her out to be with the others. She cantered off, and went to graze.

Why? Why did Cali do that? Why didn't she want to be caught that day? Did she read my mind? Was she absolutely aware that a couple of days before I'd been talking to Katie and her secret was out? Did she feel fear? Irritation? Was she pissed that I insisted on catching her that day. Why did I insist? I'd been studying really hard for quite some time by then. I was all chuffed at how far I'd got on Cali, seemingly against all odds. Had it all been a farce? Had anything been learned by anyone? By me? By Cali? If Cali could boot off Katie, what chance did I have? Luckily, winter came, and so nobody got ridden. My bruises healed, Christmas came and went, hay got blown around until spring, and it became clear I was going to have to go in and do it all over again.

3. Picking Up Glass

Our place is situated on the outskirts of a little village in West Wales called Llawhaden. There's a castle, a few houses and there used to be a phone box when there were such things. The land is six acres, which is nowhere near enough, but we get by with the help of a million bales of hay a year. Renting land for horses round here is a nightmare, because we're deep in farming country, and Welsh farmers call horses haywasters. They're not interested in anything non-alcoholic, non-subsidised or non-profitable, and so it's every man for himself as far as livery goes. The yards are expensive to stay in and full of horse people. It's easy to go down that route round here. But although I've always had that option, I knew I would never get horses until I got my own land. Of course, in the end, due to all sorts of boring details that you wouldn't care about, it didn't quite work out that way. Nearly, but not quite. We rented land, or got favours from friends, and Smurf and Delaney were moved many times together, from Whitland to Narberth, to Templeton then back to Narberth, and then, when it was time to bring Cali home, they all went together up to Efailwen. Then I had to move them again and they went to Martletwy. Eventually, we rented a field in Llawhaden, which we later purchased, after even more drama, that you probably would be interested in, but that I can't be bothered to go into. Needless to say, the process took months, it was really difficult to negotiate with the owner of the land, letters were sent, it all got a bit shouty, but finally contracts were exchanged and the field belonged to the Delismurfs.

I guess I should explain the Delismurf thing. It started harmlessly enough. On facebook, as my job I put Trainer at Delismurf Equestrian, as a bit of an ironic joke, because I didn't know how to train a horse and there wasn't a whole lot of equestrianism going on either. Still, it seemed to stick, and later on when I launched my ponysitting thing I called it Delismurf Ponysitters. We now have Delismurf Organic Eggs, Delismurf Upcycling, Delismurf Fluffy Toys; and everything is prefixed by Deli, not just by me, but by everyone who knows us. The collective term for my horses has become The Delismurfs. The tent was the Delitent, the touring caravan that we got given for free became the Delivan, and then the big static became the the Delihouse. The eggs are Delieggs, the chickens are the Delichicks, the sheep are the Delibeeps.. you get the idea.

For the whole time we'd been at the place the previous owner still had his stuff stored here. It wasn't until it became ours that he moved all the tat, and of course, it being early spring, the two tractors that towed all the stuff out left massive ruts in the grass and basically terminated all hope of a flat lawn. The mud was feet deep in places, as the field can get quite marshy when it rains, which of course provides lots of marsh grass, which Cali loves, but doesn't help when there's tons of plant and heavy machinery making its way around. Couple with that the fact that in November we'd churned up most of the top of the field by installing a field shelter, and it made for a pretty messy show. The field is weird. The top half is really wet, and most of the bottom is really dry. I've had a look at the geology and there's a clear delineation between rock formations under the ground, and it's pretty incredible how it affects the land. Little springs pop up everywhere except in the place you need them, and the streams that run down either side of the field flood over their banks in the winter and dry to a dusky stripe from May 'til October. There's lots of natural shelter, with thickets and wooded areas around the edges leading to the streams, and there are little places that I've turned into sort of dens, and named the little areas. There's Dingly Dell, South Col, Western Cwm, Eiger Nordwand, and Pamela's house.

Pamela was an elderly lady from the village who disappeared from her home and was missing for eight days. Eventually she was found with a broken neck, having leaned on a branch to cross the stream, which broke, sending her down into the deep channel and hiding her from the search parties. Our neighbour found her one day whilst pulling his tractor out from the mud, an inquest was held and a verdict of accidental death was passed. In the castle there is a bench dedicated to her memory, and she had been long since forgotten until it was mentioned to me as I sat in the solicitor's office, waiting to sign the papers.

Many people from the village insist there's a ghost, and we've had a few little goings on, yet nothing I would say that was particular definitely the ghost of Pamela wandering around. But every May 14th, on the anniversary of her going missing, and so I can only assume the day she died, I light a little candle and we think of Pamela, who used to love walking through these fields, and took a shortcut across the streams. We all know from Ghostbusters about the danger of crossing the streams (BOOM!), but in all seriousness, I wonder why a lady of her age, seventy-six, who had dementia, had been allowed to wander off and roam all by herself. I like to sit down by her tree, and wonder where she was heading for, and what she was up to, and whether she was singing a song as she imagined herself a girl again, and balanced on the tree, skipping across. To her, the path she took that day cost her life, and every time I'm in the same place, or any place in the field, I feel the same way, that even if I don't mean as much, I'd give my life for the place, in a way I have, in that I'm the girl that's slowly turning into a horse.

The more I get to know horses, the more I wonder whether I used to be one in a past life. I've always thought of myself as being more doglike, and I suppose, perhaps I was when I was young and not all broken and injured and not very cynical and before my mind deteriorated and my vitriol took over. I used to be pretty outgoing; I was an actor, a musician, I played in bands for years, at festivals and all over the country. I busked in streets and went on stage and went to auditions at the BBC and filmed in old banks in Cardiff for HTV. I went on game shows, walked on stilts, ate fire, did street theatre, circus, juggling workshops, youth theatres. I was a teacher, a lecturer, a youth worker, an estate agent. I talked on phones, kept on top, I owned a music shop. I ordered stock, set up drumkits, negotiated, bartered and gobbed off. I stuck to guns, asserted myself, wrote big cheques, marketed, swerved and hustled, paid a mortgage, brought up kids, shuffled and scuttled and eventually the whole thing collapsed on me. I lost the shop, all my savings, had tons of debt, and a couple of breakdowns. Diagnosis of BPD and severe depression, lots of meds. I guess you could say, I'd been fighting all my life to hold it all together, just like a cart horse walks a busy road, and you think those blinkers are working, and they are for a while. One day, for no reason, the horse snaps. No one knows why, everyone's confused. The horse seemed so docile. He worked so well. He's pulled that cart for years. He's never missed a beat. He was always on top, never let himself down, learned quickly, toed the line, held it together. Then one day, he bolted and off he went with his totting cart full to the brim, losing furniture along the way, throwing his shoes, tipping his cart, breaking his lungs and eventually comes to a disheveled stop, panting and exhausted, with no more fight and with no more flight. Two things will happen. He'll either lose his spirit forever, and become what people call bombproof, sold on to an unsuspecting new owner who will just be lucky to never know what happened, and it won't happen again, because the horse knows, it makes no difference. Or he'll go the other way. He'll see the carnage he caused, realise he has strength and power, and he'll realise he doesn't have to be pushed around anymore, because he's terrifying when he's angry, and to keep them all away, that's all he has to do, be really, really angry, and then all the stupid peoples scatter about, and he gets left in peace. Or so he thinks, because someone, somewhere, is preparing to have him shot. Not euthanised, because that's too expensive for a horse that's lost it and is dangerous. He'll be shot because it's pence and not pounds, and he'll drop to the ground like the pathetic creature he is, the creature fooled into thinking he had strength, but realising that against an evil world with no understanding his strength would work against him, his power would be suppressed, he would be controlled. There is no freedom, except the bullet, which he would take gladly if he knew what the continuation of it all would be. That horse is my horses. That horse is me.

When we first moved to the field, at that point, just Delaney, Smurf and Cali, it was full of glass. Broken tractor windscreens, caravan windows, even beer bottles. It was everywhere. Because it was so spread out, I had to lay bits of carpet over the areas until I could get to them and clear them. For five months, I spent ages each day picking up all these pieces of glass. Big bits, little bits, fine shards, tiny diamonds that were so small they could only be spotted in sunlight. For a year and a half I walked everywhere scanning the ground for pieces. it's all gone now, except occasionally I will find a tiny piece. Luckily, I've never found any in the horse's hooves, and no one has been cut, but of course, the glass areas had all been carpeted, which they tended to stay away from at first, but eventually just wandered over, of course, proving a happy accident. I was watching all these youtube vids of trainers and their tarps and stuff, and chuckling at the fact that my guys would walk over a carpet. They would also walk over my tarps while I was trying to put up shade shelters for them in the hot summer. I'd have them all laid out, and then they come over and sniff about and refuse to get off, like cats when you're trying to wrap a present. Of course, originally, it never occurred to me that this was a big deal, but if the likes of Monty and Klaus et al were using them to demonstrate wonderful training techniques, I thought I was either onto something, or the horse world must be really, really, stupid. From my BHS experience I'd had my suspicions, and after watching so many videos and reading so many books of what everyone had to say I was starting to go dizzy. He said this, but she said that. So should I this or that? And why do any of it when my horses walk on tarps just to be deliberately annoying? And what's the big deal about the tarps? Yeh, I know, sacking out, whatever, but…. so why do mine just stand on them? I didn't ask them to, and in fact, I'd prefer they didn't because they're just messing with the programme when they do. I even used to shake the tarp to shoo them off, which worked on Smurf, but he'd be back a minute later, hassling again, and it never worked on Delaney, who just stood there, going "haha". So yes, I know they flight at some stuff that they're not ready for, but they've got no objection to rustly things per se. And I thought maybe it was just because I'd had them since babies, and at this point they were, I guess about three and a half, and used to me shuffling around on my missions. But still. Why was the horse world obsessed with tarps? One day I jokingly said that I'd invented the art of training without training, like Bruce Lee's fighting without fighting in *Enter the Dragon*, and I called it Horsemanship by Osmosis, and that stuck too.

In a way I suppose picking up all that glass could be seen as a metaphor for the journey that was unfolding for me. Endlessly searching for the tiny pieces that would mean everyone stayed safe. Finding every danger, every hidden piece that was waiting to pierce us. I trod on a nail that was in a piece of wood, buried, in the long grass. The nail went straight through my flip-flopped foot, and I ended up in casualty for a tetanus jab. All I could think was; I'm glad it wasn't one of the horses.

4. Borderline Pony Disorder

There was an ad on facebook, Horse, free to a good home, can be ridden, perfect broodmare. Then I saw another advert on a horse site, with the same horse, can't be ridden, would make perfect broodmare. The picture showed a pretty palomino with a baby on its back. Of course I went for a look, which was silly really, because I'd just written and recorded a song called *You three and Me*, about Smurf and Cal and Del, so I was messing with things by going and looking at number four, but then, I was intrigued by these ads. She was on loan to a girl at a yard down the road, so we trotted off for a butchers.

When we got there she was in stable, seeming quiet enough as I led her out to the sand school and asked her to go out onto a circle, nice and gently. Suddenly, like a cork, she exploded into buck, buck, gallop, and proceeded to career around and around as I held on for dear life. Someone I'd watched had said if this happens, don't let go. So I held on. Round and round she went, until we got into a rhythm and because I was so dizzy by this point, I had to stand in one place and pass the rope over and over my head like a lasso. The girl she was on loan to and my husband looked at me. She's 19. I said. she's gotta stop eventually. Every time I stood in front of her driveline, like all those natural horsemanship chaps had told me I should, she just bucked. They said she'd stop. They had lied. So I wasn't sure what else to do after that. *She's clearly bigger than me,* I thought, *so I ain't gonna argue*.

Eventually, the poor old girl slowed and stopped. She stood, out of breath and confused. I stood for a while to let her get her breath back. "You finished lady?" I asked.

"Yes." She said.

And that's how I met Fray.

She arrived a week later, delivered by the owner and her friend, the girl who had her on loan had jumped out of the sand school when I'd taken Fray off her lead rope, so she was clearly glad to have moved her on. The condition was that she was not on loan, but that she was given to me. The owner agreed. The horse came out of the trailer. They'd had a pretty easy time catching her, and then blindfolded her to get into the trailer. Turns out she'd only load blindfolded. I'd never heard anything like it. Who ever came up with the idea to blindfold a horse? Is this common? I was wondering how she's got the blindfold around her ears, as Fray bounced into the field, off came the halter and over she ran to the edge of the field and tried to graze. The owner left, it was pissing down with rain, like, absolutely pissing down. Smurf, Cal and Delaney ran around trying to intimidate and investigate the new girl, and within ten minutes she had all three of them out of breath as she continued to prance around with a show ring trot. I was impressed. When I'd viewed her at her last place her hooves had been pretty overgrown. Since then someone had done a sketchy trim, but even so, the laminitic rings on her hooves showed a long and varied history of laminitis. Remember I said I'd hurt my back at college? Well, for the six months after that, I could only do the bare minimum of horse care, and it was winter, so I laid on the sofa for months watching endless videos about hooves and trimming. Smurf would NOT stand for the farrier. Simple as that. And Delaney went lame every time he was trimmed. I decided to try and find out why. As time went on and I learned more I started to trim the guys myself. It all went really well. I was able to do things gradually with Delaney, and I'd learned about abscesses and realised he'd had one deep in his frog for ages, which had been causing intermittent lameness that the vet and the farrier couldn't suss out. It's impossible in such a short space of time to see these hidden things, so I'm not dissing them. It took a long investigation to work out what had been going wrong with him. I also managed to persuade Smurf to be trimmed. He's still not keen, but he'll do them, one at a time, which again, is impossible to ask of a farrier or trimmer who is visiting. I had learned lots about laminitis, and seen lots of experimental trims, dissections, possible causes of mechanical problems and what not, so I decided that this little yellow horsey Fray would make a good hoof study. I gave her a few trims in the first few weeks, trying to make her more comfortable, and it worked. After a couple of months her feet looked great. She no longer limped, and could rest on her front feet enough to rest her back feet while she slept, which she couldn't do before. I was pretty chuffed with myself. As I watched her graze one day I realised she had bulges above her eyes and wondered if I remembered right that this could be a sign of cushings disease. Had I read that somewhere? As soon as I got home I googled it, and sure enough, there it was. I messaged her old owner who told me, yes, she was diagnosed with cushings years ago. Ok - no one told me, but then, it wouldn't have made any difference, I'd have still had her. I considered Prascend and decided against it because of liver problems. I tried chaste berry, and she instantly improved. her lethargy disappeared, her eyes began to sparkle, she was less attractive to the flies that had gravitated towards her, and she had a spring in her step. All was well with Missis Fray, and though she still hadn't made friends with anyone, and always grazed alone over on the Western Cwm, she seemed happier.

Fray's old owner's friend, the one who had provided the lift and the trailer which brought Fray home, also had a cushings horse, a little pure white Section A called Silver. She was going to have her put to sleep. She had to live in a stable alone, as the owner had a stallion, and spent her days in a small yard, shifting from foot to foot. Her feet were getting worse, even though she was on Prascend, so the owner asked me if I wanted her. By this time I was getting too many horses. I ummed and ahhed, and eventually we came to an arrangement. Silver could come and stay with us. She would have friends and poor grazing that wouldn't be too rich, plenty of room to get some exercise. I would trim her and do what I could, and give her the time the owner didn't have, and the owner would pay for the Prascend she was having, any other vet bills that might arise, and if it came to it, she would pay for Silver to be PTS in the spring if her feet didn't improve and she continued being in pain.

Over she came. Instantly, Cali tried to kick her head in, while Smurf and Delaney ran around lookin' 'ard and neighing. Even Fray got involved, running in with Cali, one at a time, like a wrestling tag team, intimidating the tiny horse, who was even smaller than Smurf. She stood her ground, and their threats increased. They got closer and closer, and then suddenly Cali went in for the kill, with her best flat ears face on, teeth bared and a spinning roundhouse kick being expertly set up as she thundered towards little Silver. Little Silver looked up, paused, looked up at the lumbering, approaching Cali monster, who was far too fat to stop herself. Cali launched, Silver turned, Cali flew, Silver kicked, and her little hooves hit Cali square in the chest. Cali stopped like.. *what just happened?* This was too much for Smurf and Delaney. In they went, fists flying, but Silver kicked them both like a spinning ninja. In went Fray.. Silver turned.. Fray stopped and thought.. I'm too old for this, and stood near Silver to graze. The others looked on in amazement, us humans laughed, and basically, everyone went home for tea. No one picked on

Silver again. Cali loved having someone even more hardcore than her around, and Fray had found someone that she liked to hang out with. They weren't best buddies, they both grazed alone, but close to each other alone. Occasionally the mares would hang out in a bunch. Smurf and Del started to love Silver and groomed with her lots. She had sweet itch and was pretty bald, and she limped, but she was muscular and strong and willful, and if there was ever a horsey that could will herself well, I thought, this is the horse. I did her feet every few days, studying as much as I could. It was getting on for winter by now, which was good as the growth was slowing down, the sugar had gone from the grass, her sweet itch gave her a break. She did really well. Around Christmas I was looking at her belly and wondered why it looked so big. I messaged her owner and asked about the possibility of her ever being in with the stallion. "Maybe," she said, "I can't say no for sure." We had taken Silver off the Prascend and I was trying her with chaste berry, but as both are considered dangerous to a pregnant horse, the owner asked me to stop both. Silver deteriorated very quickly. By January she was skinny, by March, really skinny, but still had this big belly. She had been wormed, so it wasn't that. I kept in touch with her owner, and kept her up to date, She's fine, she's well, her feet are good, but she's losing weight.

One day, late in April, Fray's old owner turned up. She made me take some pictures of her and "her" horse (I'd had Fray since early August) and had a look around at the work we'd been doing to the field. She saw Silver. "She looks rough", she said. "I know." I said. She left soon after. About an hour later I had a text from Silver's owner, asking how was Silver? I told her the same as I had been saying in my emails all winter. The next day she turned up.

The next two weeks became two of the worst of my life. The owner had gone ballistic when she saw Silver, saying she was emaciated, which she wasn't, but she was very skinny. She had actually put on a bit of weight, as I'd found a food that she would eat. She was on Calm and Condition and Veteran Mix. I had tried a million different things, which any of the feed stores around here will tell you, as I wandered in perpetually, to see "what else you got?" The old owner took photos, which I didn't even notice, as she started to get angry with me, and I started to get angry back, saying, "dood.. I've been telling you all of this…." To cut a long story short, cos it's all too nasty, she made lots of threats, and then a couple of weeks later came with her friend to take Silver away. They couldn't catch her, which I found ironic, because I'd never had a problem catching her. My friend Mel came over, my husband shouted at them, but it was no use. They eventually bribed her with carrots and dragged her up the field, as the rest of the horses went mental, and screamed out for their friend. They put her in the trailer and drove away, and Silver was gone, just like that, and I sobbed until I couldn't sob any more, and then I wanted to kill people.

I'm upset now, writing this. It was a long time ago and I'm able to drive past their place without wondering every time if Silver is still there, or if they did ever put her to sleep. I hate what happened. It resulted in massive animosity between me and her owner, and lots of slagging off of me on Facebook. Fray's owner turned up some months later and we also fell out; she'd mentioned taking Fray, and I had told her there was no way that someone who made money for nineteen years out of a brood mare and then dumped her on someone else when she was too old to breed anymore was ever getting that horse back. I wish I hadn't let Silver go, but I knew she was ill, I knew she needed treatment, and I knew I didn't have the money. I know that she was taken to a vet afterwards and had lost a third of her bodyweight. She also wasn't pregnant. No one mentioned what her feet were like. I miss Silver. I took a bullet for that horse. The first article that I had published on *horseconscious.com* was seen by Silver's owner, and she wrote a damning comment on my article, accusing me of starving a horse, and calling me righteous. I was being slagged off on Facebook by both Silver's owner and Fray's old owner. And I thought long and hard before including these stories here. But I have for a few reasons. One, to set the record straight and have my say. I've kept a dignified silence over the whole thing as much as I'm able, which anyone who knows me will tell you that's no easy feat for me. I'm pretty sure their sides of the stories would be different. And whatever side of the story you hear it doesn't stop my heart breaking that I could have and should have done more for Silver. That's the other reason these stories need to be here. It's not all flowers and roses. I messed up. It's not all success. I failed. I let her down. I did my best but it wasn't enough. And my best should have been better. It wasn't a good best. My reputation with horses was basically shot to pieces, just as it was getting quite good, and only my real friends knew the bare bones story, and Silver's owner of course, who should still have all those messages I sent that winter about Silver losing weight, like I have.

It doesn't bother me anymore that they hate me. They have their own thoughts to get over. You'll make your own decisions I'm sure. Silver hated eating. I have video footage of everyone eating hay and her just standing there. I tried for ages to find food she liked. I stood in the stinking rain trying to get her to take Prascend in a million different ways that she always sussed out. What does bother me is that I don't know what happened to her, and I hate that she might be alone and missing the guys. It was hard work being around the field for a long time. Everyone looked so sad, the mood was subdued, the sun had gone in, and there was still a pile of fur where she had rolled on her last day here and left winter fluff behind. It was there for weeks, near the Delivan, and it was hard to look at. But the hardest thing to watch was Fray, who when Silver left, went back inside herself and continued as the friendless yellow horse.

5. Unstable Vices

When my friend Lisa told me about a horse that had been abandoned down in South Pembs, of course I went to have a look. When I got to see her, there was a foal as well. Their passports had been handed over to World Horse Welfare when the owner left them, and the yard where they lived was being sold, so the people with other horses there and who had been looking after them, had to move. And so did these two. Soon. Very soon. Of course you know what's coming.

Within days of arriving, Puppet, the foal, so named because of her funny face and her ridiculous dangly legs, had eaten the field shelter that we had just spent weeks putting back up, after the crazy southerlies had blown the roof into the saplings and narrowly escaped crushing some poor unsuspecting family filled car on the road the other side of the hedge. I couldn't understand why she was eating all the wood. So I googled it. Cribbing? Ah.. so that's what cribbing is. They had been stabled for about six months before I got them, and Puppet was only ten months old when I got them, so she had really weak legs, that as I've said, were far too long. She couldn't get up hills or over the crazy terrain of the field, which was still pretty muddy, it being March.

Both her and her mum had scabs where their rugs had been, and to this day I've only managed to get a rug on Delphi once and Puppet no chance times. Delphi did a weird thing too. She would turn her head sideways and make a weird, selfie, duck face, and move her head around. What the hell is that? I wondered…. so I googled it. Wind sucking? Ah.. so that's what wind sucking is.

As we don't use lock up stables, I've never seen stall vices before. I haven't spent enough time on any of those stabley kinds of yards to see either. I did once work at a stud farm that had stabled stallions that were completely insane but that's another story. It was far worse than wind sucking and cribbing, let's just leave that there.

I was puzzled. How do I tackle this? I did some searching on internets, and the advice being given was along the lines of put metal on the stable, and tie the horse shorter, and all sorts of other odd things. I spent ages looking at given solutions, and again was given pause to think that the horse world is indeed, completely mad. I tied rubber tyres around the field shelter and replaced wood and did everything I could to stop it falling down on everyone due to Puppet's habit, as I racked my brains about what to do. And as time went on I realised that they weren't doing it as much. Puppet chewed the rubber tyres and seemed happy just to have something to chew. *Well, puppies get bones, kids get dummies, foals gets tyres. Seems fair to me,* I thought. And Delphi did the weird face less and less until I realised that she hadn't done it for ages, and eventually, as Puppet started to get stronger, and run around with Smurf and Del, and hang out with Delphi and Cal, getting as big as them and looking like Baywatch babes, that she just stopped doing it. So their vices stopped, over time, and barely perceptibly, and it got me to thinking about osmosis, and time, and stables. Again, here we were with an example of the horses learning something without being taught, and really all they learned was how to relax, and when they relaxed, the behaviours stopped. It's really not rocket surgery is it? Is it? The forums I looked at and the magazine articles I read about stable vices, or as they're referred to now, stereotypies, went on and on and on. Turns out you just gotta let the horse out of the stable, give it some mates, some grass, and a few months, and it all just gets better by itself.

Ah yes.. the months thing. You see.. this is where it all falls down. People don't want to do the months thing. They want it to all happen now, because it's eating into riding time. That reminded me; I'd forgotten to ride any horses. Still. I'd been putting it off since the incident with Cal, and decided I'd better start thinking about that next, seeing as we'd cured these vices. I wonder if we could apply the same things to this getting on the Cali monster?

I began wandering up to Cali in the field, rubbing and catching and scratching. I'd catch her and then let her go. I did that for ages. Then I would catch her and take her to the round pen and do a bit of playing around at liberty, moving her feet, like the NH boys said, and generally playing. We never did *Join Up*, and we never did much chasing around. Mainly because you try and chase one of my guys around and they'll look at you like you're a nutjob and stand there staring at you, waiting for you to start feeling stupid so you'll leave them alone. I'd lean on her back a lot, and then get her to the mounting block and lean over from there. When I first got her she was really funny about running or moving in a circle to the right. She wouldn't let you on her right side. So we worked on this side loads and loads and loads. Eventually, she stopped letting me do anything on the left. I decided to try and mount from the right instead of the left. This seemed to be a hit, and she would let me get on and get off, get on and get off, repeatedly. She stopped moving her butt away, like she had always done before, when mounting from the left and we seemed to have turned one of those strange corners. I had been doing all this bareback with a rope halter, and we got as far as walking a few steps.

One time, I tacked her up with a friend's tack, a nice Liberty treeless saddle and a bitless bridle. I tried to mount. She moved her butt, for the first time ever on the right! So I took off the saddle. I tried to mount. She moved her butt. So I removed the bridle and put her rope halter on. I tried to get on. She let me get on. It was then that I realised I had a way to communicate with Cali. I had to let her have a say, and when things were ok for her, then she would let me do the thing. That was one of the biggest lessons I learned. It led me to thinking about getting horses to do things with pressure, which I had never really been comfortable with, and I started to see chinks in Natural Horsemanship, and my questioning of it began to get bigger.

We started to walk around the round pen, and if I felt that voltage in her body, so easy to feel bareback, that she wasn't liking things, I would slide off. She seemed pleased that I listened, and let me stay on for longer and longer. I wondered what would happen if she did what she's done before, and knew with no saddle it would be landmine time. So I made the decision, against all advice, to bail if it got hairy, because I'm too fragile to be doing anything else, quite frankly. I also made the decision to dump the rope halter, because I worried that once I'd bailed, there would be this rope halter and rein attached to her. We had got as far as riding with one rein, so I wondered why we needed them at all, seeing as she turned by my leg, or weight shift. If the reins weren't there, she couldn't get tangled up and hurt herself by catching her feet or all the other scenarios that used to go through my head and make me nervous. So I eliminated all the danger that I could. There was nothing left to go wrong. If she went, I'd bail, she'd be unencumbered by ropes, and free to run, and we'd all try again another day. This process went on for months. If she didn't want to be caught I didn't make her, and I began to be able to take the mounting block over to her, wherever she was in the field, and get on. her attitude went from.. *Oh bloody hell.. again?* to.. *Well.. ok.. you get off pretty quick, you don't make me do any crazy stuff.* Eventually I could get on her at any time, no matter how long it had been since last time, in my flip flops, go for a short wander, and then slide off and go and have a cup of tea. One day after I did that I realised, I'd done what I wanted to do. Ok, so Ding and Dong weren't following romantically, although they watched sometimes, as did everyone else. I decided one day to get on Delaney and took him over to the gate. I got on. he was fine. I got on a few more times over a few more days, He was fine. I got on him in the round pen one day and Jimmy walked around with a carrot. Delaney followed him, with me on his back, no saddle, no halter, no anything. He'd never been ridden before, and here he was, at four, being ridden around, and not even really realising it. Riding by Osmosis. I'd done it.

The thing is, once I'd done it, I never did it again. I'd proved all that I'd set out to prove. To myself, and to everyone else, especially to the people who had written off Cali. Ok, so we weren't razzing round or hacking out. It was just two friends, learning with each other, but that's all I'd ever wanted anyway. And once I'd done it, and it was all easy, I didn't want to do it anymore. I'd always been known pretty much as the horsewoman who didn't ride, because I didn't do activities or ride properly. It was just me and a horse in a field, doing nothing special or spectacular, sticking to a gait of our own invention, the bimble, and spending the rest of the time lying around together. This, to the horse world, was the kind of thing that got whispered about. I was helping people with difficult horses by now, and people were starting to snigger that I didn't much ride, and I tried to get better so that I could work more with horses, maybe start them for a living or something. But it became apparent that you can't do that. You can't take in a horse and just do it in weeks. What me and Cali had been doing took ages, and if you'd put a saddle on and a bit and tried to go off riding, who knows what would have happened, and that's what people want to do. It was impossible. I began to feel like a fraud. I could understand the horses I went to see, but I had no way to communicate to the owners or riders what the problem was without offending them hugely. And I couldn't understand the owners at all. To me it was obvious. The horse may just as well have been wearing a tee-shirt with the problem on, as it was evident in seconds, and it was sometimes evident before you'd even met the horse but had just had a chat with the owner. I didn't get why I could see this and they couldn't, with all the years experience they had. But then it became clear. That was the problem. The years of experience. Years of being told what to think, how things should be done. If you learn those things too early they become too ingrained. It's an insult to question those truths. So it became impossible to balance what I believed, and what the horse industry requires. Something had to give.

6. On the shoulders of giants

You know what it's like. When you're trying to find information, you'll look everywhere and anywhere to find what you need, if you really want it. Google and youtube can become your best friends. They can also lead you up a few garden paths. I made my way through all of the gurus and the experts and the masters. I watched Monty Roberts and then read his book, impressed for a while, until I came across Rick Gore. I never got into Parelli, luckily. Who can afford that? And I thought in Rick Gore I'd found a master, and he is at what he does. He answered a couple of my emails until I asked a question or two too pertinent. Sacking out was confusing me, and I wanted to know how it worked with phobias. I'm desperately terrified of spiders, and you could sack me out all day long with a spider on a stick and all that would happen is that I'd have a heart attack. Also, one time, the night before my twentieth birthday, I argued with my boyfriend. He stopped the car on a dark country lane and chucked me out. It was so dark and I was so stressed that I literally wet myself. Isn't that what it would be like for horses, I asked? To be so scared and full of flight that you have no physical control? I couldn't find the answers to these questions and so I laboured on. I found lots about positive reinforcement and treat training, but realized you couldn't get far unless you had a billion treats with you. Also, with my guys all together, the minute a treat comes out, you get mobbed and everyone has a fight. I read about Bill Dorrance and Ray Hunt. I watched the Buck Brannaman movie, I watched a German lady do amazing bareback things, but only with a stick. I watched Bill Campanelli and loved the way he stood around smoking roll ups while guiding horses through crazy exercises, all the while looking a bit pissed. I read the books of Klaus Ferdinand Hempfling and he seemed to come really close to the way I thought. He kept trying to explain what he was doing, yet seemed to be unable to articulate his secret. His secret seemed to be that he just knew how to communicate. I found Alexander Nevzorov, the guy everyone was calling "The mad Russian" and loved his skill and control with horses. Then eventually I saw *The Path of the Horse*. What struck me about Stormy May's film, was that she had given it all up to find a new and better way. She wasn't stuck in the old way of being with horses. She respected them enough to stop what she was doing once she knew the truth. Just like Nevzorov, arguably one of the best riders in the world, gave up riding as soon as he was made aware of the damage riding does to a horse's back. You try and tell any local pony club type rider that, and they'll shoot you down. They think I'm making it all up just to be annoying. A massive cognitive dissonance sits firmly over the horse world, and anyone who deviates from the traditional way is seen to be a complete mentalist who doesn't know what they're doing. Reading Alexander's book, *The Horse Crucified and Risen*, made me laugh and cry in equal measure. I'd found someone who got it, and who was as vitriolic as me. I felt like I had somewhere to be. So I joined his forum, where I found all sorts of amazing people. It was like a homecoming. A lot of the people on there were much more gentle in their opinions than Alexander. And I tried to be patient and serene like them, but found it too hard.

The thing that's worked for me, is a recent collaboration with Stormy May. Getting to know her and doing her course, *Compassionate Communication with Horses,* has given me the tools I need to quiet my angry mind and to become more accepting. When my neighbours were giving me grief at Darklands she suggested taking them a pie and making friends, whereas I was thinking more along the lines of poo through the letterbox.

I thought I had seen freedom in the Pignons, but it was still control. I thought I saw it in Monty Roberts but seeing his show live in Bristol made me realize he was a man of the circus. Way ahead of what came before him yes, but way behind what has become apparent since. In Alexander Nevzorov, I found the purest distillation of horsemanship. And he gave me permission to be the horsewoman I'd always wanted to be. I gave up working with other horses and adopted the philosophy that the horse is always right. I didn't even desire to follow Nevzorov and some of the other students into LEP or into Haute Ecole elements at liberty. And that was ok. There was no prescription. Help and learning if you wanted it, but no prerequisite or insistence that things are done a certain way. The first and foremost consideration is the horse, and it becomes a lifetime's work to discover all we can about these creatures that we choose to spend our lives with. There's a Facebook page called friendship training, and if you're on there, telling a boy off because he posted a picture of himself with his horse where neither of them are wearing any shoes, and you're telling him to be careful of his feet, then to me, you've missed the entire point.

7. Tycho

Sometimes, you end up getting involved in something. And one day, a sudden panic will hit you and the oh shit moment will occur, where suddenly, it all seems like a really, really bad idea. That moment happened about two weeks after meeting the big blue stallion. Tycho.

You're getting the idea by now, that it all started innocently enough. I got word about a horse that was too crazy to move, that needed to be moved, quick sharp. He had been kicked as a foal by his mother, moments after being born, and the well meaning owner, an ex-riding school owner, took him away and put him by the fire and tried to get him to eat. He refused to suckle, and she gave him buckets of milk. apparently he was injected with some substance by the vet when he came, a substance that was given to soldiers returning from Iraq. I have no idea if this is true, I've never heard of such a thing. But apparently, it made him jump up and wake up and become little mister energy. He still wouldn't suck a bottle, but he would drink from a bowl. And so little Tycho grew. Eventually, when he got big, and was by now very boisterous, a little gypsy vanner colt, he was sent outside to live with the mule. And that's where he stayed for two and a half years. And then I turned up.

The owner had been trying to give him away for some time. I just went up to see if I could help, and as he bounced around the corner and I saw him for the first time I saw that he was a beastie. He approached, opened his mouth and tried to eat everyone. The owner put her hand in the air and he licked her hand then tried to eat her arm. "No one can get in the field with him." she said. "One girl tried but he tried to mount her. He hasn't been touched since a foal." I stepped back as he tried to eat my clothes over the gate. He leaned and leaned, his crazy head movements reminding me of Delphi and her wind sucking. The owner shrugged. "If you can get in there you can have him."

The horse had calmed a bit and looked at me in stillness. His eyes looked sad, like they'd been drawn on with cartoon like angles. His forelock covered the other eye. I went towards him. He tried to eat me. I blew a raspberry at him. He stopped. He tried to eat me again. I blew another raspberry. He made the funny, sucky face, so I did it back. He stopped and looked at me. He still looked sad. *Oh shit..* I thought.

A couple of days later Jimmy came with me to see the boy. I thought it best to take him, as if I needed an ambulance I might not be able to get to the phone as my legs were being eaten and my head was being played with like a Jollyball. The owner came up to the gate with us, and in I went. The boy bounced towards me like one of those scenes from *Jurassic Park*, where the dinosaur is running towards the terrified guy who's just about to get eaten. I raised my arms and he screeched to a halt in

front of me. A beat. Then he tried to eat my clothes.
I blew a raspberry, he stopped. I scratched his nose.
he stopped. I scratched more.

Peace….

There he is, there's that boy. Hiya boy.

He let me scratch him some more then came out of
the trance and lifted his nose to bite me.. I blew a
raspberry. The poor guy just stood, looking
confused. I thought this might be a good time to
quit while I was ahead, so I tried to sidle out of the
field. He came after me and tried really hard to
munch on me; Jimmy came into the field and
distracted him, and so he went over to Jimmy and
tried to bite him, so I distracted him with a rope I
had in my hand, letting him chew it for long enough
that we could lead him over to the gate and get out
of the field. *That boy needs a dummy more than
Puppet ever did,* I thought.

"He's a hooligan." Said Jimmy. "I loves him."

"So do I."

Jimmy sighed hard.

"Ah Shit." he said.

We couldn't move him yet, because he was
entire, and with four mares at home, that was just
asking for trouble. So it was agreed to wait until
autumn when the flies had gone, and spend the next
couple of months getting him handle-able. By
November he was tame enough to be gelded, and
the day after I took him home. To get him in the
trailer I filled it with nice things and let him walk in
and out a few times by himself. Eventually, when
he was all the way in and calm, I quickly shut the
ramp. He went totally berserk. I jumped in my truck

and drove him home, 9mph up hills in my crappy 1.6 petrol Vitara, which shook as he kicked at the trailer walls and left dents. The wibbly-wobbly Maenchlochog roads gave way to the home stretch and eventually we pulled up at the field.

Everyone else came to see who had arrived. Tycho had gone quiet in the trailer. I opened the front ramp and stepped back quickly. Tycho jumped out like he was master of the world, ran around to try and bully everyone and instantly got beaten up by the crusty mares. They walked off and left him, totally unimpressed. Pedro and Trotsky, the two rescue Shetlands that we had recently picked up came over and made friends. Smurf and Delaney showed off a bit and went off to be with the mares. The previous owner had called him Harvey but I changed his name to Tycho, as it seemed to suit his large, heroic frame a bit more. But standing here with his new tiny friends, he really looked more like a Harvey.

Getting around the field became a bit sketchy. You needed to keep something with you as a shield. I settled on carrying around a piece of old tyre. It stopped Tycho from launching in for a bite, and also provided him with something other than my head to chew. I still have the lumberjack padded shirts from that time. They are all shredded and eaten all the way up the the elbows. One day under the tree, Tycho decided to launch over at me. Taking me completely by surprise. Instinctively I called out "Delaney, help!" and Delaney, who had been a few yards away, instantly came over and started to fight Tycho off. They reared together and scuffled like stallions and I stepped well out of the way, amazed at this incredible display, and even more amazed at what had happened. Was Delaney really saving me? Why? Did he see me as one of the herd? Or did he say to Tycho… "Jesus mate, calm down. No Tesi - no carrots; think on't!" Either way, I was pretty glad. And from that day on, Tycho calmed right down. It was like he had learned his place. The mares still bullied him, and as his recent gelding began to take effect he slowed down even more. He became a puppy that followed me around the field. He became good mates with Delaney, and they hung around together, hassling me as I worked around the field, getting in the way and nicking my tools and walking off with them. They'd come walking into the workshop as I was trying to fix an engine, and knock everything onto the floor that I'd laid out in order. Then they'd stand around in there, taking up all the room until I paid them some scratchy attention. Tycho became, essentially, best horse. He'd still have a nibble at times, or give a playful bite, but only to play. He still does sometimes. And when he's stressed he regresses. But he's a perfect example of why you should give a chance to a hand reared horse. Everyone was impressed. "Amazing" they all said. "He's a different horse. You're a genius." Of course, I could have told them all immediately that it wasn't me who made him normal, it was the other horses. But I left it a little while, and basked in the smoke being blown up my ass.

8. The girl who turned into a horse

Eventually I sold my house and moved to the field to be with the horses. A change in personal circumstances made this necessary, but I also wanted to. I had no electricity, no running water, and lived in a caravan, eventually having to move into a bus when the council got shirty. I've had an enforcement notice, I've sold the field and we're moving on to somewhere less freaky. For the four years the horses were at Darklands, and for the nearly two years that I lived here, we have all become one and the same. I used to hate the storms, knowing that the horses were out in it. Somehow, me freezing along with them in an act of solidarity takes away my guilt, makes me feel like we're all in it together. By the same token, the summer months can cause their own issues. At one point during last summer we were down to 100 litres of water between me, the animals and the garden. My pak choi bolted, I was super grubby and unshowered, and when it rained we all did a mega rain thanks dance and swore we wouldn't waste water so badly. This is something you don't get when you live in a house. I had been taking water to the horses every day for ages, and it was hassle, but it was do-able; I had a tap at home. But here we were all in the same boat, or desert, as the case may be. Our water supply is collected from the roof of the field shelter and filtered. Our electricity is provided by solar panels. So in the summer you've got tons of ellecy but no water, and in the winter you've got tons of water but no elleccy. But it's ok, because it's all of us in it together. When it's muddy, the horses get muddy, the bus gets muddy cos the cats and the dog are muddy, and I get muddy, the chickens get muddy; basically everyone looks like they're singing off the same hymn sheet. Sometimes I don't realize how grubby I've got until I'm chatting to a very clean person at the garage and I compare their general colour to mine.

I've always had a touch of the agoraphobics, but now it's impossible to leave home, especially when it's sunny, and you want to get on with garden missions, or when it's rainy, and you want to watch crappy documentaries. I got right into Breaking Bad but kept running out of electric. Now that was a pain in the ass. Sometimes you just want to live like a human for a while, and be in a centrally heated place with an electric kettle and SKY. But I have Netflix, plenty for me, but yes, irritating when Walt is just about to kill someone else and your batteries go dead. The inverter makes an irritating pipping noise when the batteries are really low. The rest of the time the stupid fan comes on so you can't hear what the peoples on the tele are saying, and you can't plug your tablet into the stereo like you would at home, cos that uses too much elleccy. You become so aware of everything you consume, of everything you use. You see how much water and electricity gets wasted by living in a house. You just notice it when it's literally on tap. It's one of those things that we take for granted. We like to think that we're energy efficient, but just a fridge would wipe out my batteries in a night, not to mention the power the massive inverter uses to run something like a fridge or a washing machine. I plugged my washing machine into the generator once and was so fascinated at doing laundry somewhere other than the launderette that I watched the entire cycle, which incidentally used 7 quids worth of petrol. Ridiculous.

You can have the perfect life, or the life that you want, but you've gotta be prepared to rough it. When people ask me why I don't ride my horses, I simply reply that I don't ride my hamster either. You can tell how old the line is because my hamster has been dead for ages. But it shuts people up. I've gone from a kind of Cali horse type being, all angry and annoyed, to a Fray type being, all old and mellow and not wanting any problems. A lot has changed since we've been here together; the most ironic being the deaths of Puppet, then Delaney, then Trotsky, all during one year. Losing those guys was like losing arms and legs, I hate to say it, but especially Delaney, as he had been one of the originals. He'd taught me so much. He'd kept me sane through allsorts. It was difficult to get over, and still is now. The deaths occurred in 2016. The year we voted out of Europe and the Americans voted for Trump. It's a mad world. But the hoomans, they can have that life. I like to just sit here with my horse and cat face homies, and Valentino, my toothless dog, eat the stuff we grow, mooch around, and breathe the air. Life is too short to be anything other than a horse.

9. End of Act One

There are loads of people like me, I know there are because I've met them. There are loads of scared people. I've met them too. I've met the people who secretly don't want to ride, whether through fear or because it hurts as they get older or because they've been frightened by a fall, but want to continue a relationship with their horses in some way. A friend of mine broke her back falling from her horse. As soon as she was upright people started asking her when she was going to get back in the saddle. I find that pretty cruel. I know people mean well, and the age old adage is that you cowgirl up and get back on, as discussed when Cali launched me to high heaven. I was lucky. I fell more easily than my friend did, but it had been exactly the same kind of accident. People say that horses are unpredictable. But they're not. They're the most predictable animals on the planet. Assume that at any moment they could revert to flight animal, and accept that. With the advent of social media and instant news, we hear a lot more about the deaths, accidents and tragedies that happen all over the country, all over the world, where someone has fallen. It often turns into a campaign to wear a riding helmet, and invariably the report reads that the accident was a total surprise. That the horse bolted for no reason, that it spooked at something, that a car came too fast. I suppose you've noticed by now there are a lot of references to death. I don't really know why that is. I think because you really can't have one without the other, without wanting to be morbid, it's impossible to think of horses and death completely separately, even if it's in the way they remind us of our own mortality, and what it means to be either free or not. We forget that these are not hire mopeds. The people who went to riding establishments were taught that the horse has to do what you say. I know of a riding school that PTS any horse that plays up, kicks off, or asserts itself. Every riding school I've been to has ponies that bite and kick. they are smacked soundly, and told off. The horses that survive riding schools or yards are the docile ones, the ones that somewhere along the way lost their spirit. I have never seen a happy horse in such an establishment, and I will be lambasted for saying such a thing. I'm just a layman. Don't take my word for it. There are many books on equine psychology, on behaviour, on the horse itself, just as many as there are on riding, and competition, and how to do this or that. One only has to read the works of Marthe Kiley-Worthington to see that much study has been done. The work of Lydia Nevzorov and NHE, the studies of eminent people who have made it their life's work to study horses, from the horse's point of view. I don't make this stuff up to annoy the horse world, to be controversial for controversy's sake. I don't want to hurt peoples' feelings or take their pastimes away, but I do want them to take those blinkers off, and have a look around at what's going on. It's an uphill struggle to change traditional attitudes, and there aren't many worlds more traditional than the world of horses. Their history is so tied up in that of man's beast of burden that it seems impossible to let them be anything else. People tell me I'm cruel, because if horse riding was banned, if racing was banned, if competition was banned, if equine sport was banned, if the big money pastimes were banned, then all the horses would be put down. Really? That makes *me* cruel? The fact that the human race's answer to a large population on non profitable horses would be to shoot them all like deserters and *I'm* cruel? They'd be disposed of for being of no use? And *I'm* cruel? So many people say to me, I couldn't afford to keep a horse if I can't use it. Is that the only reason to keep a horse? To use it? Ride it? I hear people say that they don't want to get their horse a companion, because it would be less dependent on them, conveniently forgetting the twenty-three hours a day that they DON'T spend with the horse, and not even wondering for a moment what he gets up to during those times, and what he's thinking, or what he feels. A man told me once about the horses that are too old to teach riding at a local riding centre. They are taken to the abattoir. Sometimes they're so afraid when they get there that they lie down in the van and refuse to move. They're dragged out, to where they can smell the death of others, and subjected to the same fate. No vet comes to put them down gently, no one is with them. No loved one, no friend. Just the menial man who works at the yard and who gets spoken to like a piece of crap by the riding instructors. I heard it many times. They are the masters, and he's the one that does all the real care, the real work. He's the one that takes them to where they have to go. He's the last one they see. No one else at the yard gives them a second thought. They're loaded and they're sent away, and that's the last. They spend twenty years teaching horrible little kids to ride. They spend twenty years politely not killing all the little shits that come through those doors. The kicking, screeching, entitled, jodhpur wearing Verucca Salts, who are taught by heavy handed, large framed ladies, or blonde girls with angular hips and chewing gum, where the perpetual song is tighten your reins, tighten your reins. Everyone talks about contact but no one knows what it is, and the sorry business goes on and on, the machine continues, day after day, and they all, if asked, will tell you how much they love horses. Forgive them, Epona. They know not what they do.

One day when I was driving my truck out of the field, Delaney followed me out. I jumped out of the truck and rushed to the gate but it was too late. By this time, Trotsky, Cali, Delphi and Puppet had all followed him out. When Del saw he was in good company he trotted off down the road and they all followed him! So of course I followed too, on foot, and finally caught up with them all grazing in a hedge about half a mile away. It's a single track country road, but often used by cars and farm machinery. Most of the roads around here are the same, so people are used to them and tend to drive quickly, which was giving me a nice dose of worry to carry with me.

I had no tools with me, no ropes, or sticks or anything, so I grabbed a hazel branch from the hedge and used it to help me drive them all back up the road, and to guide them into gateways when cars came and tried to pass. The drivers were looking at me like I had the weirdest herd of cows they'd ever seen! At the top of the road there is a fork. The three mares went the right way, but Delaney and Trotsky went the other. I had to think fast, so I ran around Trotsky and sent him back towards the mares. I'd opened the gate to a neighbouring field on the way down, with the intention of sending them all in there, because I couldn't leave my own gate open, due to the fact that there were four more horses clamouring to be out with their buddies. Luckily, I know the guys so well, I knew that if Trotsky went with the girls and Delaney found himself alone, he'd follow. He was too far away for me to chase and get round.. I'd have just driven him further away. So I followed Trotsky and the mares and got them all into my neighbour's field. Delaney stopped, thought about it, and then cantered down to be with the rest of us. With relief I closed the gate, went back to my yard, found a bag of carrots and took it to bribe everyone home. I got a rope around Delphi's neck and led her, and everyone followed us and the carrots. I'm so glad that my guys can always be relied upon to follow a carrot! The whole event was less than forty minutes, but it felt like much longer. So the moral of this story is, it's possible to walk out with five horses at liberty, but I wouldn't recommend it.

In that moment I saw that I had been through it all, tried it all, and realised I can't really be arsed. I don't need to train my horses. To do what? All I really need to know is that I can lead them home.

10. Any Other Business

While all the above was occurring, I had a little website and used to keep a blog. These are some of the posts from that blog. The attitudes within them are different from the attitude I have now, but broadly, I still feel the same. These little blogs show the process of my understanding, and taken in context with everything else they help to explain how you come to the point I've got to now. These blogs are no longer online as they were from my old ponysitters page. So I reproduce them here, so that you can see the rest of the puzzle. I look at these blogs now and I was so naïve. I had absolutely no idea what the hell I was doing most of the time. But if you believe in something, you can make it happen. My mantra is, and has always been; "Whatever Works".

"Horse Training is a process, not an event" - Rick Gore

"For me, it was never just about riding the horse" - Klaus Ferdinand Hempfling

There are many schools of thought in horsemanship, but the most crucial thing in these times is that people are starting to listen to their horses. In the age of information overload from every conceivable angle, we are exposed to the thoughts of and opinions of people we could never have previously heard from; everyday people from all walks of life, and not just the published, the famous, the mainstream. My form of horsemanship I once jokingly termed Horsemanship by Osmosis, but as time went on I realised that it is in fact just that. I never went to pony club. I never had formal riding lessons. I never got a winter pony on loan. I watched as everyone around me did all of those things, but somehow in my heart, although I knew I wanted to be with horses, I knew I had to wait for an alternative way to do it. A lot of ponies lived in our village, and I would go and watch them for a very long time, and then I would just go home.

My mum used to work for a company selling cavity wall insulation, and we would spend every Saturday in a caravan in a town centre selling insulation as I sat with my crayons. Invariably this meant that sometimes we would have to attend the Holt Show, or the Royal Bath and West, and I would watch with envy as my mum's boss's daughter competed in the gymkhana. Not because she was competing, but because that horsey was all hers. I would come home and put belts on my bicycle handles and use them as reins, which meant I would fall off my bike. I also had reins on the gate and would swing back and forth. My grandad always promised that when he won The Pools he would get me a pony. He used to call me Vicky, after the girl on Black Beauty, because that's all I ever watched. I even had the album. Of course my grandad never won The Pools, and I never got a pony. Of course, now I have lots of ponies, and Black Beauty brings me to an interesting point. Those stories.. they were very far fetched! I remember one episode where there was a Black Beauty evil double, and it would do bad things and Beauty would get blamed. Of course, Beauty saved the kids and exposed the bad men and it was all fabulous. But the way the kids reacted to the "bad" horse was completely the opposite of what they should have been doing. If one of them had known for one second what they were doing, they could have exposed the bad guys a hell of a lot sooner, and probably saved the evil double from the meat man. But of course, that wouldn't have been a very good story. But wouldn't it? Wouldn't it have been a good story? I think it would have been a fantastic story. Picture this: The children understood the horse, they stayed out of danger, the audience learned something about horsemanship and the bad guys didn't get away with it for as long as they did. Beauty wouldn't have had to have that fight by the tree, therefore avoiding his injuries, and the bad horse could have been rehabilitated with a bit of kindness and understanding and gone to a nice family in Surrey. Beautiful.

There are a lot of fantastic horsemen and women out there. The latest vogue for so called Natural Horsemanship has caught on in a big way. There will always be the staunch traditionalists, but the winds are changing. Kelly Marks is now favoured by the BHS, Monty Roberts worked for the Queen. Buck Brannaman has a film out of his own and is mates with Robert Redford, Klaus Hempfling is able to command massive fees for his courses and people will pay, because what he does looks like magic. Nevzorov is causing controversy all over the place with his no riding stance. The Pignons are wowing half the audience and filing the other half with things to worry about on horse forums. There are many forums where some extremely entertaining arguments and debates are raging as we speak. One controversial figure, Rick Gore, had over 600 hate posts dedicated to him until recently on horseforum.com because of his methods. Pat Parelli is famous for his horsemanship, his controversy and now, his wife. Clinton Anderson and Chris Cox are making a fortune with their own shows on channel 280. Everywhere you look there are courses and clinics. You can train online with Carolyn Resnyck or Horse Whisperer Missy Wryn or John Lyons. You can become accredited. You can come to Wales and become a qualified horse behaviourist in just a few days. We have schools of horsemanship termed Natural, Traditional, Authentic, Classical, Savvy. We have the Alpha Male, the Alpha Mare, the Passive Leader, the dominant relationships, the affiliative behaviours, the clicker treats, the positive reinforcement, the negative reinforcement; you can do it how you want and call it what you want. Take a path and stay there, or learn from everything. It's all out there for the taking, as well as the continuing popularity of the BHS stages and exams, the only route into the closed world of riding instructors and most livery yards and stables. But the BHS misses one vital thing. You will learn a lot about husbandry, bandages, anatomy and feed, but there will be no answers to be found when Neddy decides he'd like to refuse to load, kick you in the head or throw you to the ditch. There is no horsemanship training in the BHS. When a horse plays up his back is checked, his feet are checked, his teeth are checked, but if there's nothing wrong, then the horse is often labelled a bad horse. In some other forms of supposedly gentler horsemanship other problems occur. The horse becomes a puppet, a remote caricature of itself. The dominance idea caught on just a little too much, The halters became a little too severe, the devices a little more exclusive, fashionable and expensive. In replacing one doctrine another appeared, and the quest for the most distilled form of horsemanship continues. That's what I'm seeking. I may make some enemies here, but I also hope I make some friends. I know I'm not the only one who wants to see things from the horse's point of view.

To me, the term Horsemanship by Osmosis completely encompasses my modus operandi with my geegees. I believe that the best way to be with a horse is through time. We are so time deficient in our lives that it's difficult to achieve. In times past a horse was a constant companion, used for work and transport, and they weren't the luxury items they are today. But only through time spent with your horse can you see who he is. In a herd, with his pasture mates, that's the closest you'll see to wildness in a domestic horse. So many vices are caused by unnatural keeping practices, and some are necessary for the type of work that people want or need to do with them. I see so many stressed horses that it breaks my heart. Top level dressage horses for instance are invariably and unquestioningly assumed to be nuts. What came first? The dressage or the nuts? There are so many people out there looking for answers with their horses, but the simple answer is that there is no one answer to cure a particular problem. It's a trust issue, and without trust the whole thing falls apart. But how do you build trust? Time. That's how. By being a leader, by knowing your horse, reading his body language, learning how to communicate with him. He is not a hire moped. He is an animal. A smart horse often gets labelled as a difficult horse because he may protest. He may become dangerous if he is not heard. He may end up being passed from home to home and may never be understood. Horses are about as complicated as men, and by that I mean that you can choose to overcomplicate them extremely easily. Theories on herd behaviour are rife right now - there are as many theories as there are horsemen or women. And that is the point. We can only see what we see, take what advice we can take, try everything and see what works, and come to our own conclusions. I use a mixture of treat training, love and affection, kindness, patience, and lots and lots of time. I never have an agenda. I let them know I love them and will never hurt them. I show them I know what to do if there's trouble. I show them they can trust me. I show them that I trust them. Being trained in theatre is actually really useful. It's all exactly the same thing. You're dealing with all the same issues as a horseman as you are as an actor. Fear, subtlety, body language, status, reactions, improvisation, relaxation, flexibility, fluidity, communication, physical skill, timing, concentration, feel, trust. No one understands subtext like an actor or a horse! We want our horses to love us. But they don't have the concept of love that we do. They respond to cuddles when they feel like it, but most of the time that's just pressure. It's a privilege and not a right to touch a horse's face, yet so many people will just mindlessly put their hand in a horse's face, and then call them grumpy when they don't like it. So many people don't understand that their new horse is afraid, frightened, misses his old friends, hasn't been accepted by his new herd, needs to find out where he is in the pecking order, find his place. He can't know his place if he is in a stable and alone, or when he's cared for by lots of different people. There will be difficulties, and that just has to be accepted. I believe that building a relationship with a horse is like any other relationship. It has been said that if you see the horse you see the person. That a horse is a reflection of its human. If you're having problems with your horse, the answers are out there, but there are no specifics. There are many techniques but no absolutes. A horse must be absorbed by you and you by him, like an actor assumes a role, putting it on like an old coat, knowing it inside out, its faith, its fears, its hopes, its courage, it's limitations, its story. When an actor knows all that, he can bring his character to life. If he doesn't, his character will be wooden and lifeless. John Lyons once said that there are no horse problems, only people problems. An actor who doesn't study his part will be transparent to all. 90% of horse problems can be cured very quickly, by learning your lines, studying your character, quelling your fears and having the confidence and courage to go out and give a good performance. If you do that, the audience will believe you. And so will your horse.

Don't Touch the Ears

We've all heard it. Don't touch his ears. I can't touch his ears. My horse hates having his ears touched. You should never touch a horse's ears because they don't like it. Ears, ears, and more ears. Specifically, I was told once by a very experienced I've run a livery yard for thirty years type lady that her horse, her "baby" that she'd had for 28 years would "take my head off if I touched his ears". I touched his ears. He left my head where it was. The lady got angry. "Well, he usually does." Is what she said. And you know what? I suspect he did usually did, you know why? Because she expected him to. And how many people had put that myth in her head at the beginning of her thirty years, and made her expect the self fulfilling prophesy that resulted? How far does this stuff actually go back? Well.. we know.. it goes back as far as the domestication of the horse. Read the works of Nevzorov to see the full appalling history of our relationships with horses.

This proliferation of lies, of myths, of expectations. Where does it all come from? Here's one of my favourites; I hear many people say that horses are unpredictable. These are people that have spent a lot of time around horses. How can they still think that horses are unpredictable? Did someone tell them that and they just mindlessly repeat it with no thought? Because anyone who spends five minutes with a horse can see immediately that they're among the most predictable creatures on the planet. So what's with this unpredictable stuff? Do you mean, he kicked you while you were talking to Sue and you weren't watching what was happening? Is it that he bucked you "for no reason"? If everyone who "spends time with horses" actually spent time with horses, there wouldn't be these myths.

I've been experimenting with my herd of numpties, because let's face it, their job is to let me experiment on them. So, as most of my guys are youngsters, I've been playing with their ears from day one, without making any big deal about it, just as part of the find the scratchy place game. And guess what? They ALL love having their ears scratched and played with. Even the old crusty mares that hated it before like it now, even Tycho, pictured above, who was too dangerous to play with for a while, has adopted it as his new favourite thing, which suggests to me that horses, like hoomins, like to have their ears scratched, and it's hoomins that are making horses hate it.

So what's going on here hoomins? Why is this occurring? Could it be the same kind of thing as asking why your stabled horse cribs and weaves all the time? Or asking why your ridden youngster barges everyone? Or panicking because your late gelded colt is "mouthy" and biting the crap out of you? Have a think before you repeat something you heard, and see if you can observe that behaviour in real life. And before running off onto the internet and googling some random question and either believing the first divvy you come across, or confusing yourself with a million different answers that can all be in many ways right and in just as many ways wrong, ask yourself the question, and then ask your horse, and see what they've got to say. Because if you thought about it for as long as you think about what hat or breeches or show clothes to buy, you wouldn't have to ask.

Wot, No Ponio?

So, George... you've been duffing up the taxpayer in order to rustle yourself up a little paddock. Whoever is interested can happily peruse today's Guardian and see all the facts and figures for themselves. This is I'm sure, pretty old news and I guess all that's happened to bring it to the fore again is that facts and figures have emerged that prove what we knew already; that we are being fleeced.

Is it just me or is the collective helplessness of the nation beginning to be on par with the learned helplessness of the equine? The Common Man is becoming as much of a victim of circumstance as his horsey counterpart. We are led by fools, treated like idiots, bribed, conditioned, observed and fiddled with and left in the shit, all the while our owners enjoy their lavish existence, their relaxing security, their untouchability. We can only look on from our muddy fields, observe the lack of grass and sigh. Luckily for horses, some of them have good owners, that bring hay, that study, that learn to know their horse, that treat him as a friend.

We humans have no such luxury. Who is coming to save us? Everyone got on the Russell Brand wagon for a bit, but then he started to dress up like Jesus and it all got a bit silly. He's not the Messiah, but he's a very silly boy. He nearly had us there. Then we have Anonymous.. are they coming out to save us on Nov 5th? Is the fact I refer to them as THEY, tantamount to me giving up and deciding that life in a field full of chickens and horses is about all my over 40s head can deal with? I went on every protest march going as a kid and, as the Young Ones referred to us sardonically, a "Young Adult", but now my energy has gone, my fight has left, my apathy is huge, except when it comes to the world of the horse. I guess it's essentially because I don't know what I can do about the human condition, but there's something I can do about the horse one. One likes to not feel overly helpless in these matters.

And there I think lies the key to the healing nature of horses, the honesty which they represent. There is no lie because they cannot. There is no farcical sense of helplessness in their company and there is no crass attempt by them to pull wool over eyes or anything else. They are the most transparent, and predictable species in the world.

Alexander Nevzorov talks at length in his book, *The Horse Crucified and Risen,* about Jonathon Swift's Yahoos in *Gulliver's Travels*. I won't repeat. Go and read both books. You'll be better for it, horseman or no horseman. In terms of the horse world, we see the overindulgence, the control, the need to rise above a lesser being. In human terms we see this in our parliament. Attempting to rise yourself into some kind of historical juggernaut, you fleece the Working Man in order to buy the status symbol of all status symbols. A paddock.

And the greatest irony, the greatest insult, and the greatest indication of not only the deluded and empty mindedness of your average politician, and the emptiness of his soul, his pointless posturing and his absolute inability to follow through with an idea, he didn't even get a horse....

FYI, or, The Delismurf Commandments

Ok - here's what I'm going to do. I'm going to print this out and stick it on my gate.

1. Yes, they are rescues. That's why there are quite a few of them and some of them are a bit lop-sided. They weren't test ridden, hoof kicked, vet checked or assessed in any way. I bunged them in the back of a van and brought them home cos they needed somewhere to be.

2. The ones that you want to report as being lame are, actually, lame. One has cushings, one has EMS. Occasionally they limp. Occasionally they get abscesses. However, when they got here they could barely walk, so any limpiness is an improvement. An occasional limp doesn't mean I should put them to sleep, so stop telling me that it does.

3. Yes, I have bought the land. The mud on the road is from the old owner moving his stuff and using tractors to do it with. The shit left behind is the shit he couldn't be bothered to move. It is not my shit. It will be burned, tipped or made use of all in good time. We are between exchange and completion. Calm down.

4. I am not a gypsy, although I find that a shame,

because if I was you wouldn't dare to talk to me over the hedge in the way that you do, because you would be scared to. Please note however that I do have some gypsy friends. I'm also chummy with quite a few Hell's Angels. Please bear this in mind when you see fit to be overly rude to me, as all you deem me to be is a scruffy, muddy girl wandering around alone carrying too many buckets.

5. I am a knowledgeable horsewoman who deals with problem horses on a daily basis. I am training to be an equine psychologist. I research what is best for the horse and I base my care on that, not on what Dierdre at the yard told me, cos Helen told her and Mrs Yard Owner told her cos that's what the BHS said. I have no preference as to which hand I use to groom, I don't ever use tail bandages and I call hooves "paws". I have no care for the mainstream horse "Industry". I don't give a crap about dressage, breeding, bloodlincs, competitions or telling anyone who's boss. This does not mean that I don't know what I'm doing.

6. My horses live naturally. This is different from neglect.

7. They don't wear rugs because they don't need them. When they do need one they get one.

8. I am with them every single day, for as much of the day as I physically can be. I don't just turn up once a week to ride. I am involved in their hoofcare, their healthcare, their nutrition requirements and their training. No one does any of these things for

me.

9. Pyjamas are more comfortable to work in than jodhpurs, and nothing you say is going to change my mind on that. I don't like uniforms, and don't need a Mark Todd logo to make me feel like I'm "horsey".

10. I'm here to stay. Deal with it.

Contending with the Fretful Elements

The weather is so rough right now here in West Wales, that it's hard not to worry about the guys in their field. But the truth is, even though the new shelter recently went up and they could, if they wanted to, hang out in the dry, they seem to be actually staying as far away from it as physically possible.

In other news, the Delitent has finally given up and collapsed. My poor kettle has now been rendered homeless and everything else has had to go into the shelter, so I guess in a way it's lucky the horses don't want to be in there, although I bet you a crisp pound note that as soon as Delaney realises there are things in there I don't want him to get, he'll be in there, getting them. I'm actually rather enjoying this weather. I like the fact that horses force you to go outside on days you would never dream of going out on given the choice. But the howling winds always sound worse and the rain is never as heavy as it looks from the inside. It's exhilarating to be pushed around while your boots stay where your feet used to be. It's amusing to be in the middle of a bunch of hungry horsies while they sort out the issues you've created by carrying buckets around with you. It's good exercise carrying hay miles across mud and poop flats because the wheel barrow can no longer cope with the terrain. It's interesting to arrive at the field and see that the trampoline is upside down and making its way towards Wiston. Yes, I like this weather. Much better than all that "I can't breathe" nonsense that we had in the summer, where myself and the guys would splay ourselves around in the field, too exhausted and harassed to move, and gazing in wonderment at the trotting horses that passed by the field and wonder how either rider or horse could be so hardcore as to even move.

I'm in my cosy lounge right now, but the window is wide open behind me. Tomorrow morning I'll be back out there, getting soaked, getting too hot in my much too waterproof padded strides, getting the evils from Cali, cuddles from Del and Smurf, indifference from Fray and Silver Spook, and planning how to rebuild a 50 year old canvas tent. Life is good. Merry Christmas humans. See you on the other side. ;) x December 2013

Sea Horses

I got my husband a tropical aquarium for his birthday, just a little one.. and man, I am sold! I love it! I've never had fish before, not even a funfair fish. I had some in a pond once but you barely saw them. These guys are lit up like Blackpool at christmas, and I really, really like it.

I often tell people I treat the horses as giant goldfish, because I spend such a lot of time just looking at them and relaxing. And the similarities are huge. Beautiful, elegant, silent, movement... it's all there, but I realise the fabulous thing about fish, is that you can go and get more. They cost pence, there's no one to say, "seriously..another one?" you can get as many as you like, tank permitting, and when your tank is full you can get another tank! Loads easier than getting more acres and building another shelter. Their food costs £2.09 and will last around 6 months. They don't like hay, they don't get laminitis and you don't have to go out in the rain to look at them.

Fish also have advantages over the other pets I have. No digging up sawdust and throwing it around the house to be hoovered up by me like the hamster does. No secretly pooping behind the tele like the cat does. No making a stinky litter tray and meowing at windows. No woofing in the night and insisting on going out for walks every time you sit in a certain chair and make a certain movement, like some repetitive Pavlovian nightmare. No ballistics when someone knocks at the door, no tripping you up on the stairs. No perpetual meowing first thing in the morning until you get the food out, no standing on the backs of your flip flops every time you try to run up the stairs. No cutlery, bin bag or hoover neurosis, no nonchalantly weeing on the cupboard while they look you in the eye and wonder what your problem is, no chewed up socks, no missing shoes, no muddy paws, no running around a wheel at 4am, no cow eyes every time you try to eat, no scratching at the back door, no worming, de-fleaing, vet's bills, hoof trimming, catching, training, saving from the dog warden or apologising to farmers because of. Much as I don't resent the constant barrage of annoyance from my mammalian chums, I rather like the easiness of these colourful and unobtrusive new additions.

Yes, I think we can safely say, I like fish. There. I said it. I know it goes against all my usual principles to like pets with no fur, but I feel I have no choice other than to concede.

Off now to google the psychology of tropical fish. Later humans. X

Lonely Man

Whilst out and about today I came across a little pony in a field all by itself. Of course I stopped, and gave him a carrot, and tried to generally give him some company for a little while.

Why do people do this? Why do they keep a pony alone? They are herd animals. How fundamental do we have to be here? Without other horses they are afraid, they don't sleep properly because no one is looking out for them. They never get to lie down and have REM sleep. They are afraid of predators and have to be aware all the time, a situation which leaves them stressed and exhausted. They get bored. They get lonely. They can't perform natural instinctive behaviours like grooming and playing. And this was a young horse, probably not much older than a yearling, with no one to teach him to be a horse, or protect him, or make him feel safe.

I hate that I'm usually really negative on these blogs, but I just see so much that inspires me to write, mainly because I need to get it out of my system, but also to let anyone who is listening know that it's wrong, and maybe persuade someone they know to get a companion for their lonely horse, or get one for their own lonely horse, because maybe they didn't know any of this. Well, now you do know this. Don't keep a pony alone. It's more than cruel. And if you're having problems with your horse, and it's kept alone, then that is why. There are free horses everywhere at the moment. Take one in, give it a home, and give your horse a friend. They will love you for it. Promise.

Forty-Eight Hours And A Couple Of Quid

I hear about a lot of unwanted horses, but this week one in particular has struck me. I had seen it advertised for sale for very little money, and there seemed to be no interest. I then spotted that it had become free to a good home, and if it wasn't homed it was going to the sales. Now, I don't follow the sales, so I didn't know that the one at Llanybydder was on halloween, and that there were only 48 hours to urgently find this lady a place to go. So I hear you thinking.. free horse? Surely it would have been snapped up.. even as a very cheap horse it could have been snapped up, but this girl's problem, and the reason that no one wanted to re-home her, was this; She was completely unhandled. Not so rare for a young horse, but this horse was 11 years old, and was a brood mare who had, with the present owners, had three foals. It ran wild with the stallion in the field, so I'm guessing its pregnancies followed on one after the other. There was every possibility therefore that she was currently pregnant. She still had a foal at foot who was weaned three days before the sale. Anyhoo, bit of background for you, before I tell you what happened. I got involved, as is my wont, as I didn't like the idea that this poor lady, after many years of service and bearing foal after foal, was going to be stuck in truck, taken from her baby and put in the ring to be bought by, well.. I don't know.. the meat man in all probability.. at best, a home where someone was looking for a project, but then they'd probably prefer a youngster, or a companion, in which case it would need to have some kind of handling skills, which it didn't. Not even a little bit.

Not only did I get involved, but a lot of people did, trying to find it a temporary home. What transpired was that I got three people interested in taking her on. Without going into too much detail about the hoops people were trying to jump through to help, one needed more time to sort some land, one needed the horse to be handled before her yard would let it be there, and one needed a companion horse but couldn't take one until the end of november. So.. I jostled my landlord and to my amazement he said I could take the girl on temporarily. So I organised a trailer for sunday (the sale being on the thursday) informed the potential new owners that I was willing to take her on and make her handleable, and then go from there. I mean, it was a lot more complicated than that, and there were other potential homes and lifts and stuff and going ons too, but that was basically it. So, You're thinking.. cool.. so the owners gave it a couple of days and then you went and got her right? Well - on any other planet you'd be right. But you know what? They damn well took that horse to the sales anyway, with no clue of who was gonna buy it, whether it would fall into good hands, be a friend, glue, or Chappie by the end of the week.

So yes, you are right.. let's remind ourselves. There were three potential homes, all good homes, willing to take on this pony. I was prepared to go and get it, my friend was prepared to drive us up, the potential new owners were prepared to chip in for expenses of going to get her, and I was going to give the poor girl a start by getting her used to a halter, being led, handled, touched, fed, feet checked, able to administer medicine to, able to be loaded, and generally give her a future during the time she was going to be with me. But instead, the owner, who had gained three foals from this lady, couldn't give it two extra days in order to guarantee it a more stable future. Now, I know that there is every possibility that this dear girl went to a good home, and unfortunately of course she's one of many that ends up at the sale, from no fault of their own, but because stupid, selfish, profiteering humans can discard them when they no longer need them, conveniently and quickly. A beautiful horse will quite possibly be dog food by tomorrow, along with many more who were at that sale. Because no one handled them, no one gave them a life, they just took, and kept taking.. right up 'til the end where they took the measly few quid that she would have ended up selling for. I keep trying not to think about where she is right now, and how she feels, and how her foal feels. They will both be terrified I'm sure, but not as terrified as I am, by this heartless cruel world that we seem to inhabit, and which petrifies the crap out of me. Those poor guys can see their bad situation immediacy for sure, but thankfully they have no perception of the hopelessness of a selfish world; no nihilistic thoughts taking their attention away from that bit of grass by there.

I hope that they get over their wounds, as my guys have got over theirs. And I hope they find a future, even if the human race seems so determined to persist in its profiteering cruelty that it insists on careering towards anything but. Yes, the world is terrifying. There are plenty of horses who don't get the chance, and the owners really do have no choice. But to know that your horse had been offered a secure lifeline, after giving you service and doing your bidding, and to not take that offer... All for the sake of 48 hours and a couple of quid. Brutal. Shocking.

I understand that some people may take offence to this article, and you know what? I don't care. The situation as it is offends me. So now, as Hugh Grant once said in a certain film, after also offending pretty much everyone, I need to be somewhere where people are not.

Horse Thefts And The Theatre Of The Absurd

Daily, on my Facebook newsfeed, I see stories about horse thefts in the UK. Also, I see multiple posts about abandoned and homeless and fly grazed horses. I see that native ponies can't even fetch 10 guineas at auction. What's wrong with this picture? Who are these phantom heartbreakers that steal into a paddock, pick a pony, drag it from its owners and then what? What are they all doing with these horses? I saw a post today of the theft of a laminitic horse, obviously laminitic as it was wearing a grazing muzzle when it was stolen. Seriously? There are beautiful horses abandoned and being given away all the time. I was recently given an old girl who's last owner could no longer accommodate her due to life changes. I get offered ponies and horses for free all the time which I can't take on because of lack of land, much as I'd like to take them all in and read them a story. Smurf and Delaney were thirty quid! I don't have to go out and nick horses.. they're blimmin' everywhere! So why take someone's much loved pet when there are thousands of ponies all over the countryside who, if taken, would hardly be missed, or possibly no one would even notice. I don't get it. You can go to auction and pick up a pony for pretty much nothing, even a rideable one can go for peanuts, yet somehow, pot luckers in trucks are nipping round picking up anything vaguely horsey shaped. Two very distinctive greys were stolen recently, Section A ponies. One, the fact that they're so recognisable is daft, and two, the fact they're only big enough to be ridden by the under 10s is daft too. It's not like they're bagging Shergar is it? There's not going to be a reward and a public campaign. With free horses everywhere, who are they going to sell them to? These poor owners are having to rely on social networking to try and find their beloveds. Some ponies are microchipped but still don't make it home!

New laws have recently been introduced in Wales regarding fly grazing. I suspect there is going to be a lot of beautiful stock surplus to the requirements of those that leave them all over the place, on bits of ragworty land with no grass, no water supply, no worming, no foot care. Please, potential horse thieves, if you're reading this... for ten guineas (about £10.50) you can pick up a New Forest Pony, or for even less you can grab yourself a fabulous Gypsy Vanner from the edge of the road and no one will bat an eyelid. You'd be doing it a favour as it would probably be heading for the abattoir anyway. Please leave the loved horses with their humans. It's cruel to the horse, it's cruel to the people who lose the horse; it's just cruel. If you want them for meat, then there are auctions for that, and they are seriously going for pence. Think. Do the right thing. Don't take someone's friend. And if you do, well, I damn well hope the bugger bites the crap out of you.

Treat Training And The Sub-text Of Cali

"If you want a friend, feed any animal" - Jane's Addiction

I saw an article this week on facebook posted by *The Horse* magazine. Research had shown that horses can clearly remember a trick they were taught two years previously, without any retraining, but if you didn't give them a reward for it for a few times in a row, they would stop performing the trick. The conclusion of the study was that horses have good memories, and also that they're not stupid. This got me thinking today. I originally had to teach my guys to pick up their feet using a combination of patience, treat training, and cunning. However, still, some days, Missis Cali, and occasionally Mister Del, get a bit of beef about them at hoof picking time. So today I introduced the Paws for Carrots campaign, inspired by the research I had read about. As soon as everyone clocked that there would be a carrot in it for them after only lifting two paws.. (yes two.. not all four!) then there were no issues and they were actually offering their feet. Cali was the only one who took a while to catch on, but Cali always likes to have the last word, and doesn't ever, ever, ever, like you to know that she's complying in any way. She'll comply, but only when she can pretend that it was all her idea. She truly is a study in horsey subtext... Anyhoo. The treat thing. Many people say don't give treats, many people swear by them. Clicker training and other forms of positive reinforcement and training of other species, such as dogs, rely pretty much completely on food rewards. The Pignons, Hempfling, and other wizardlike horsemen clearly train their guys with treats. But yes, it's true that horses can get all treat pushy. And this, as always, is a dominance and herd pecking order issue. As I'm having to give Fray chaste berry, I'm having to hide it in feed, and so I have to give the other guys feed to make it fair, and now of course when I arrive they come running towards me, manes flowing, and I stand there in the wind pretending to be the kind of warrior princess that has four horses spontaneously wanting to be with her, and not a scruffy, muddy, socks tucked into boots small town girl, dressed like a cross between a blind clown and a farmer. So, the consensus? Treats... Good idea or not? Do you treat your horse? Does it cause problems? My guys fight so hard over food sometimes I swear they'll hurt each other, but that fight for dominance is being introduced by me, the human. I'm messing with their programme. In the end of course, I'd like to reduce treats to an absolute minimum, which I did for a while, but it was true.. their little tricks and obediences did start to slide; questions were asked, unions were formed. We hoomans don't expect to work and be given no reward, and for animals that think with their stomachs, (and that includes all four of my greedy "good doers") it's definitely an incentive that I am willing to utilise. I can pretend that they all stay close to me because they all love me so much, and not because I smell of apple. I can pretend that when they come when called and follow me around like puppies it's because I used pressure and release. Well, of course, sometimes I do.. but this is loads less hassle! Years ago, horsemen and trainers used to carry a product called Pax to keep the horse interested in them. Like a kind of horsey catnip. So long as I am always their leader, and they see me as such, I don't see the harm, although I do see the benefits. And not just to me, but to them. They look forward to the odd morsel of noms, and who can blame them? I'm sitting here writing this and I'm half way through a 200 gram bar of chocolate. Go figure. And, I bet you a crisp pound note that even though Cali played up today, the minute she sees the Paws for Carrots stall going up tomorrow she'll be offering me her feet like a New York socialite in Manolo Blahnik. Will let ye know..

Mud and Loan Homes, No Mention of Rugs

Hi there hoomans... the rain is getting ever more frequent, and one little Smurf pony in particular is very happy about that! Officially a palomino, Smurfie usually looks more nicotine yellow than anything, but today he has been playing army ;).

On facebook today I saw a post offering a pony for loan for the winter that needs "bringing on". Now I don't want to offend anyone here, but doesn't the translation of that seem to be, "I don't want to go out in the dark and cold and look after this horse that's no use to me, would you feed it and keep it safe, and while you're there would you train it and bring it on for me for free? And next summer I'll have it back and I can ride it." Doesn't it say that? Am I just being too cynical? I have never really been able to understand the concept of a loan home. I can see that maybe in certain circumstances it might be a good thing, owner ill, can't look after horse, horse needs to do what it's used to, willing rider can benefit and so can horse, etc etc.. but so many loan homes wanted ads seem to be a way of blagging free livery. Too controversial? I won't mention the rugs then.. I'll leave that for another time.

Gimme Shelter

Finally.... The guys have a shelter.. in a nutshell. This will be Delaney and Smurf's fourth winter together. Their first winter was before I knew them, and they shivered on a hilltop overlooking the bay at St Davids. Lovely view, bloody freezing. Short hedgerows, baby horses, just weaned, just saved from the sale, wild and cold and I can't continue or I'll blub. The next winter they were with me and lived at my friend's place in Templeton. 30 acres with lots of horsey friends to hang with and tons of natural shelter. A good year. Last year we were in Martletwy, in a windswept field facing West, with one good hedgerow and Missis Cali as their only guardian. A cold winter that cost me a bomb in hay and had me carrying it across two muddy fields with a slipped disc. It was awesome. Finally, we are where we were meant to be, and they are with a proper herd, what with the addition of Lady Fray and also with little Silver Ghost Spookie over on sleepover for foot rehab. Three older mares to watch over them and kick their butts, and finally, a run in shelter, that they've never had before because I've never been in a position to be able to build them one. Standing in there today, as they totally ignored it from the other side of the field, I thought about how lucky I am to be able to finally give them what I need; my peace of mind. Yes, I know, I said what *I* need. But that's basically the selfish truth to be fair. I know that as Delaney spent all summer trying to move into the Delitent with me, that by next summer he may well be interested in hanging in a cool place away from the flies, but so far, even though it's cold and rainy and a bit rubbish outside, they're still not particularly interested in their new bedroom. Ok, so there's only been a roof up for one day, and it's only half a roof. And the floor is still wet, and there are tools still kicking about, and yes, we haven't finished. But I was kind of hoping they would run in, snuggle up and get the cards out. However, they're doing what they usually do, and ignoring all my efforts to spoil them.

The RSPCA say it isn't essential to provide horses with shelter. I believe it's absolutely essential. All summer they have used the trees to their advantage for shade and rain cover, and now the trees are mostly bare, and only going to get barer. I'm sure that once they get the hang of the new shelter, and once the floor is dry, and there's straw, and some nice hay, and some other forms of bribery, that they'll be vying with each other for the best space. But the main reason it's essential for them to have a shelter really and truthfully, is because now I can enjoy winter again. Before I had horses, I spent winter indoors and cosy, jaunting with the dogs but predominantly becoming a hermit and looking out of the window feeling warm and happy, with the odd thought about the birds and the associated guilt being relieved by the provision of peanuts. Job done. However, since getting horses, every rainstorm, hailstorm, windstorm, snowstorm and thunderstorm have been spent freaking out because of the "poor babies" and generally making myself into a whining bore to my family and friends. This year, I am happy. I know that if they choose to shelter somewhere dry, they have somewhere to go. And if they're standing in the rain looking melancholy when I rock up in the morning, it's because they are choosing to be wet and melancholy, for effect, and for more carrots probably. It is my birthday next week and I will be 41. And it's true what they say; life really does begin at 40. I actually, finally, have pretty much everything I want. I am a very lucky middle aged bint, and I know it.

Ok, So I'm Irritated Again

Whenever there is any kind of discussion on a Facebook page or forum about horses, inevitably some bright spark always comes along and says "if the horse didn't want to do it he wouldn't".

This phrase is one of the most irritating, mindless, naive, pointless, ridiculous, insane nonsense notions out there and every time I hear it I nearly have a stroke. Quite aside from the fact the level of ignorance of the concept of learned helplessness seems pretty much entirely universal, it's also a display of the most selfish basic assumptions any human being can make. Do those twelve year old Thai prostitutes do what they do cos they like it? Or is it because they've been forced so many times that they give up? Why don't they fight back? Why don't they argue with their abusers and refuse? God's sake.. if they didn't like it they wouldn't do it. Would this comparison make people think, consider and realise a bit better? Man, I'd love to think so, but I'm not holding my breath.

We all know the horses that fought back when being made to do something by some human or another. He's the horse that no one wants and that was labelled dangerous. He's the one that will be sent to the abattoir because he's no longer suitable to be a riding school pony. He's the one who is deemed dangerous and unsafe.. he is beyond help, a maniac, a bad horse, a mean horse... he's a killer, a monster. How dare you show spirit horsey! If you do you will be punished, if you comply you'll be given a stinking carrot. And you will learn to take those tiny treats and bit of comfort when you realise that's actually all you have. Your human will come along, ride you, compete on you, and marvel at the photographs and the rosettes and won't even notice how beyond the vertical your head is, or how hard they're pulling on that mouth.. but don't complain for Christ's sake, you stinking dangerous horse. Oh.. and another thing; cattle trucks are obviously cattle trucks, sheep trailers are obviously sheep trailers. We know what they look like, we see them all the time. And guess what, we know that your horsebox is a horsebox. There is absolutely NO NEED at all to have HORSES emblazoned in three foot high letters across the front. I have never, ever once seen a cattle lorry declaring COWS in massive pink super font.. and I do not have a huge sign on my car that says CHICKENS, DOGS AND THE OCCASIONAL SHEEP. Anyhoo - haven't deliblogged a while.. been a bit too busy and a bit

too happy! In a bad mood today, so I'm back ;)
Missed me? Much love x

ABOUT THE AUTHOR

Tess has too many horses, too many cats, and an aversion to getting up in the morning. She's horrendous with money, likes toys and sustains herself almost entirely on nice hot cups of tea.

Printed in Dunstable, United Kingdom